# FREE VERSE EDITIONS

Series Editor, Jon Thompson

Free Verse Editions represents a joint venture between *Free Verse: A Journal of Contemporary Poetry & Poetics* and Parlor Press. The series will publish three to five books of poetry per year. We are especially interested in collections that use language to dramatize a singular vision of experience, a mastery of craft, a deep knowledge of poetic tradition, and a willingness to take risks. As its title suggests, the series is oriented toward free verse, but we will happily consider poetry written in traditional forms. Collections should have individual poems published in well-known journals. We will read collections that do not have a track record of publications, but it is unlikely that they will be accepted for publication.

For more information about the series, visit the website: http://www.parlorpress.com/freeverse/index.html. *Free Verse* journal is on the Web at http://english.chass.ncsu.edu/freeverse/

# Signs Following

Also by Ger Killeen

*A Wren* (1989)
*A Stone That Will Leap Over The Waves* (1999)

# Signs Following

Ger Killeen

Parlor Press
*West Lafayette, Indiana*
www.parlorpress.com

Parlor Press LLC, West Lafayette, Indiana 47906

Cover art : Giorgio de Chirico. *The Seer*. Paris, winter 1914-15. Oil on canvas, 35 1/2 x 27 1/2" (89.6 x 70.1 cm). James Thrall Soby Bequest. Used by permission. Digital Image © The Museum of Modern Art/Licensed by SCALA / Art Resource, NY / Art Resource

Printed in the United States of America
S A N: 2 5 4 - 8 8 7 9

Library of Congress Cataloging-in-Publication Data

Killeen, Ger, 1960-
  Signs following / Ger Killeen.
    p. cm. -- (Free verse editions)
  ISBN 1-932559-21-3 (pbk. : alk. paper) -- ISBN 1-932559-29-9 (adobe ebook)
  I. Title. II. Series.
  PR6061.I35S56 2005
  821'.914--dc22
                              2005030571

Printed on acid-free paper.

Cover design by David Blakesley

Parlor Press, LLC is an independent publisher of scholarly and trade titles in print and multimedia formats. This book is available in paperback and Adobe eBook formats from Parlor Press on the WWW at http://www.parlorpress.com. For submission information or to find out about Parlor Press publications, write to Parlor Press, 816 Robinson St., West Lafayette, Indiana, 47906, or e-mail editor@parlorpress.com.

For Kate Saunders

# CONTENTS

# ACKNOWLEDGMENTS

I would like to thank the editors of the following periodicals and anthologies in which versions of some of these poems have appeared: *American Poetry Review, Cyphers (Dublin), Hubbub, Fireweed, Portland Magazine, M Review, Calapooya Collage, Continental Drift, The Oregonian, From Here We Speak (OSU Press), On The Counterscarp (Salmon Publishing).*

During the writing of this book my life and work as a writer has been immeasurably enriched by friendship and intellectual engagement with many people—Ken McCormack and Carol Saunders, The Casbah Artists, Carlos Reyes, Gabriele Hayden, Carolyn Mitchell, Duane Poncy, Patricia McLean, Sandra Landers, Will Bohnaker, Kathleen Ellyn, Annie Callan, Saba Hussain, Eileen Mejia, Ron Tatum, Paulette Switzer, Ron Lovell, Tom McNamara, Brian Doyle, Martha Gies, Sally-Ann Stevens, Ray Touchstone, Ciarán O' Driscoll, Noel Bourke, John Ryan, Máire Kerrane, John Eustace and many others. My students at Marylhurst and Linfield have been a special inspiration, particularly Nancy Garvin, Amy Sunderland, Sophia Farrier, Tina Carlone-Wood, Marianne Klekacz, Willow Teegarden, Troy May, Christine Linscott and Lynn Palmer.

Jon Thompson's editorial eye has been nothing short of brilliant.

My thanks to all of you.

# I
# NEW EARTH

# FERNS IN SNOW

At the cracked mouth of the alder wood
the field has lain down,
stretched out under the snow's rumpled sheet.

The tented fern-clumps are erect,
breasting the numb air.
The wind moans its lack of a body:

oh, it says, oh, when it wants to say
*Bearsfoot, Hartstongue,* I have known you
forever, *Floating, Resurrection,*

I am mad with your names.
The wood's bones rattle and grind.
                    Afterwards the silence is absolute.

# Lemon Balm

Unlike public history, the history of private life proposes
something of order, if only the durability of our senses.

In light of the world it is always before dark and after
dark, and the colorless lung of time is always heaving its
fevers and chills outwards in no very predictable way.

Fevers and chills.  Corrosive airs.  They catch in the slats
of the jalousies behind which, on an old, sumptuous
fourposter bed, a man and woman are making each other
moan
loudly and softly.

And how easy it is to trust the lasting essence of the
flesh: they walk together early, out of the dooryard where
the herb garden is in unshowy flower; and to crush a leaf of
lemon balm against her cheek he stoops into the fourteenth
century, a mist of blue-white petals, the works of Pliny, a
Book of Hours.

High summer, and she is wearing a floral print dress cut in
the peasant fashion, he, a loose white shirt and jeans.  She
inhales the lemon scent and he inhales her and tells her how
Pliny thought lemon balm so potent a bunch tied to a sword
would
stanch a wound even as the sword cut.

From far away a ripple of bells.

Now, it's not just another case of abstract warring with
concrete but what particulars
incandesce in the thin atmosphere of concepts.  Love, for ex-
ample; as when  we say "love of country" and "make love".

So, as the plague rages through Lombardy and Umbria the
flower of the young nobility seals itself inside the safety
of stories of the body's unquenchable thirst for the body,
and as the plague rages, a world-weary man in the city of
London turns from a window overlooking the Thames and
thinks
of
    *Hir fresshe beautee and hir age tendre*
    *Hir myddel smal, hir armes longe and sklendre...*

and as the plague rages they walk in from the dooryard, sit
together, drink coffee, turn on the fan, read to each other,
and, around noon, race back to their bedroom, children
running home.

# STONE CIRCLE

It is its own edge, though being
solid it lacks the precision
of an idea, and time's slippages
hunker it ever closer to the earth.

A riot of brambles flinches
at the boundary, and breaking
my way through, small birds hive off
like radar blips to the blue distance.

What persists in these stones is nothing
like memory or history:
in the local mind they're dancers
cursed to rock by the words of a saint

angered at their seduction by movement
and the thrill of the wind on their flesh.
Here no sorrow of repentance,
no silenced forms tensed for a liberation

that will never come. But
singing: the stones in their stillness
tattering the wind's glassy esperanto,

a song of *"Here, here, here is what you need*
*of the welling power of a language*
*locked to place; here is where gods are brought*

to bask in the fullness of thorns; stand here,
let your shadow's secant grow
with the failing light,
*cut us, cut past us."*

# Bamboo Flute

When you were the only green thing
in my whole yard:
that winter every storm
struck up a rattling like bones,
how at every blast
you bowed down to the fierce world:
it was all I carried
off from you till now, the bowing and bowing
to what happens here;
the bowing and bowing
since you can never tell
what will become,
what will become of you,
what you know.

I clench my lips in a kiss,
blow.

# Blackbird in Rain

(for Gabriele Hayden)
In the dream that preceded the rain
a hiding among the acid buds
of the Pleiades, a mood
that exalts a morning from the beginning.

Then it was raining, raining, raining deep
inside the day's gauzy, historical codes,
enough to make me follow you down roads
lovely and clear and untensed as the hope

of heaven. Your beak, yellower than a sun,
tinged every wetted thing with the same need
for that inward falling that ends up outside—
the longing that rises up before your song.

It came humming, my own map,
out of all your coming and going,
branch to bush, no to yes, light to pain
and back. What choice but to leap

as you leapt into verb beside my throat
and my silvery self flew in the gap
between the first lightning and the thunder clap?
The sky was the color of you, and your note

all day, all day, all day, all the unending
inexhaustible instant of your happening.

# Explorer's Gentian

Now fever burns through every village
and at night the last embers of belief
throb towards Antares and Betelgeuse.

Day is the same; the tended flax
down there in the valley repeats
the cloudless sky as a prayer.

And soon whoever remains of the women
will batter the fields into sail-cloth,
winding sheets, and flags.

A slow dance
as I pushed into the glassy air
the brief purple remedy beyond

a bitterness at the root,
a bitterness in the leaf
that is neither hoping nor despair.

And you, traveler among visions of angels,
have only to drag yourself up
where this mountain crooks its finger

in the emptiness of heaven; from the snow
that folds us under its wide wings—
mortality.

# Wolf Skull

An amber glint in the woods had already
driven up teeth of grass; eye-holes picked so clean
of wanting, it stared down the trees and sky.

It must have followed me back to the wounded place in my
dreams. I see it drinking at the green pools thin
rains of meteors distill in the tracks of ideas whose trails
are centuries cold.

Outside sleep, it satisfies
its hungers on the very thought of me.

When the moon rises it can open
its jaws to breaking and know
past reason my howl for it all the dark long.

# Sweet Basil

The man in the mirror has been
practicing concentration.

This morning in the misty rain he is picking
the last basil leaves, picking the leaves in ones and twos,
listening to the little ticks of each pluck and
smelling the basil-smell.  If his mind should wander
there is the gathering song he has made up to bring him
back to his thumb and index finger, the delicate
pressure, the quick pull, the dropping of the leaves in
the wooden bowl.

\* \* \* \* \* \* \*

*Das Kapital*—a blossom of righteous anger. In the Greek alle-
gory of Poverty a woman in rags stumbles along a rough road
clutching a sprig of basil in her left hand.  Basil,
from *basileus* meaning *king.* "Thus shall the
proletariat walk the shining path to freedom having
torn the monarchs and the millionaires from their fetid
beds".

But in days thick
with the vegetable opulence of summer it is easy
to make resolutions of simplicity; to take
a little from the earth, to reach after
*eigentlichtse Armut.* Which is a worse deception.

\* \* \* \* \* \* \* \*

The herb fit for kings,
"basilisk", the three-headed monster whose merest look
would kill.  Even smelling the plant could generate
brain scorpions.  It was probably a metaphor,
something like "agenbite of inwit", the mention of which made
you think of
children starving before a table heaped with food.

* * * * * * * *

He dreamt he was a king
who had lost his fortune and this lost treasure
was guarded by a basilisk.  But he was not afraid for he
knew that the beast's look was powerless if one walked
toward it backwards, keeping it in view in a mirror.
But the monster opened its three mouths and sang
the king's own gathering song, repeating it over and over,
each time at a higher pitch, until, at the last
singing, on the last note, the mirror shattered.

The monster's heads
moved with the deliberation of tank-turrets; in the little
piece of glass its eyes were wide with hope.

# Petroglyph of a Woman, Clo-oose, British Columbia

### I.

Moon-headed, empty-faced,
breasts hollowed, ageless
hips rounding a natural fissure--
the gluttonous, dominating sex-cleft:
Could I meet her, eye
to loveless eye
and not believe an unhuman
thrust in human generation,
a stony armature underneath
the pert flesh of Botticelli's girls
and all the other writhings
in the history of desire?

### II.

The heaving Pacific
like a blood-flecked lookout.
A hard drizzle and the air
tasted of salt as the spring tide
gushed through
a narrow channel to spume and hiss
on the cove beach.
Running my fingers in her gritting opening,
half-aroused, half-ashamed, eyes closed
trying to body forth a lover
and coming up empty.

### III.

Her hard gaze cuts away
above the rhythmic ocean,
the receptive bay, past
the white moon's averted eyes
into the teeming star-fields.
Force, energy, principle--
words cold as space.
She stares
me down millennia
past marriage-clasps, trysts, heraldic
accommodations howling ruts
in god-filled woods,
past veneration,
past self-temptation and unbelief,
and not giving up.

# Changing Direction

Trekking North-
wards, past the slate villages,
the stonefields cropping a thin wheat.

A gashed region of fogs
and scarps, the wind umlauted
that held the wheel of raucous shags.

Lungs give out
beyond the nest-holes of the auks
of Outer Elsinore.  The air

rippled with the blue whin-trees
of Almeric's Fire
in the dark days,

the dark nights, the sea-
ice scrooped against river-ice,
narwhals caught and dying.

This was not my country
though my tender quivering
was a response triggered to the wild

bony names of the hard earth.
Yet, by the sun in my compass-rose,
there should be apples, foxglove, pearly evanescent.

# RECLINING NUDE

Spring trundles back
on its twittering chariot
armed to the teeth
with tumid spears of fescue;
but she has taken her own
sweet time, making a head-rest
of her dress and lying down.

All around her body
the grasses hone their tusks
against her small shadow
but nothing can touch her;
she has planted her face
in the angle of her arm, and sleeps
while every wasting sun
rises and goes down
behind the white arc of her hip.

# THE DIFFICULTY OF BEING

## I- *Good Work*

The painter gave up drinking
five years ago, and his work gets better
beyond all expectation.  The sad thing is
most of his old friends no longer come by
in the afternoons for wine and sympathy,
though he still keeps a few bottles under the sink.
 He is working on a series of watercolors
of the bamboo trees at the far end of the garden;
some show the whole tree, others a few branches
and leaves; there is even one of a single blade
on a stem; all of them, though, are offset
in various positions and degrees from the center
of the paper which he either leaves white or fills
with an ochre wash of greater or lesser intensity.
 It is these regions of pure space touch him
with a quite sexual frisson, so that moving
his brush over them he feels he is pleasuring them
with his hand, or, unpainted, with his looking.
He plays with the idea of calling each work
after a woman,
but thinks better of it and numbers them 1 to 10.

## II- *An Affair*

All the bamboo
paintings sell and in a month the series will disperse
across four states to the buyers.  At the opening

he allows himself to be seduced by a young art student
who says she owns one of his earlier charcoal nudes
which her parents gave her on her twentieth birthday.
 Her small apartment, with its mixed smells of soup,
turpentine and cigarettes, reminds him of the old days,
and when they make love (he has made her undress
slowly while he watches) he surprises her and himself
by his passion and stamina, being older than her father.
 He stays all the next day and night; they eat
a good dinner in a Vietnamese restaurant on Sixth;
he meets a few of her friends; he says
encouraging things about her oils.  After that
there are only a few letters back and forth.

### III- *From his essay on Botticelli*

What our time lacks, and what the Florentine
Renaissance possessed in abundance, is the sense of
"the difficulty of being", to borrow Cocteau's phrase.
The term is meaningful to us in that it describes
one psychosocial condition of present-day Western
existence with its innumerable personal and social
choices, its ambivalence towards artistic work, and its
deep scepticism towards all-encompassing explanatory
principles; for us, the difficulty of being is the
difficulty of deciding who we are and what we can make
of ourselves and our world.
    But for Botticelli the difficulty of being lay in
knowing with certainty what Being is, and in being
conscious of humanity's exile from that primal
plenitude.  His high degree of naturalism is never
without a numinous substratum, an art which is
simultaneously a grieving for the loss implicit in
worldly particulars and a rejoicing in the possibility
of a restored beatitude beyond sublunary existence.  In
his earlier years this was a productive tension in that
both these poles of being held equal claims on his
sensibilities.  His later years led him to the harsh
asceticism of Savonarola, which lost him to painting. . . .

## IV- *Torso*

He believes a third dimension adds nothing
to meaning, but when he finds a big hung of cedar
thrown up on the beach he sees a woman's torso in it
and decides to carve it.  His hands become sore,
but after a week or so he is growing callouses
which please him by their down-to-earthness.
He thinks of his chisel as a kind of conduit
from his life into the grainy darkness of the wood,
his sculpting as an investment of memory.
Soon he is calling it "her" and a twist in the waist
convinces him she is a dancer, though he has never
known a dancer intimately.  He wonders if his memory
has been warped by some unconscious longing.

After he finishes the sculpture he goes back
to paint (he is doing watercolors of nudes),
and he finds himself asking the models he engages
to hold themselves in the attitude of the cedar torso
before taking up the positions he prefers,
lying or sitting down.  None of them can quite manage
the exact twist of the dancer, and every failure
fills him with the purest joy.

## V- *His poems about the bamboos*

Not yet a Buddha,
    The wind keeps tickling awake
the grave bamboo.

\* \* \* \* \*

The bamboo reaches out
    From the white fog.
Dead man's ghost!

\* \* \* \* \*

The woman sleeps
       but the bamboo won't shut up:
the long night.

\* \* \* \* \*

Through the bamboo grove
       the rain comes down.
Another day of desire.

# Tradition of the Swallow (I)

Gritty smoke from idols.

A shadow spreads on your upturned faces
and palms me back.  I could fall

so easily into the wide open arms
of grasses, but catch

in the weavings of your mythy nets
with the moon, the wolf, the rainbow. . . .

*******

Body proffered
to your widening eyes,

body unnamed
in the holy rigors of your first knowing,

on the stripped lap of your language
two catching fire together.

# Tradition of the Swallow (II)

Nothing is exact.
Warped by the roundness of your eye, I
breast a lake, churning water that holds out
hope of a congruent distortion:

the eternal algebra of curves
that must be my wings
that must be my own eyes

*******

In the ungoverning of your tongue
I am one atom of the ashes

from which you will breathe your phoenix.

# WHEN THE BIRDS FALL
# SILENT AT NIGHT

Rafting in from the Pacific
on every breath of wind: the reliable breath of rain.
Birds are the rain's cantors:
jays before rain, voices ragged from beseeching;
sparrows after, anxious, startled,
not knowing which way to turn;
and during, the varied thrush
piercing the screen of rain and trees
with her long, unvarying song.

At night, then, when the birds fall
silent, you would think the rain
should come as it comes, without ceremony,
attended only the sounds of itself,
stopping or not; but the rain won't have it:
some small parts of us wake and call beyond
reason from the woods and thickets, pleading,
and lamenting, and praising.  We're
left with the untranslated bits:

scarecrows copulating at crossroads,
wolves dancing on the roof...
In the language of birds
the lion beds down with the lamb
and the heart with the heart. Such
singing as the rain begins
and stops and again begins!  Beyond hope
the body opens like a door.

# La Petite Mort

O, O, and again
O-- the littlest elegy
for what of ourselves we lose
in one another, what we give
up willingly of our wills
to tidal heavings
in the fossil-gray dark,
pitched, necessary stars
caught int he nights
of two far countries,
each the other's promised home
since so many million years
ago, we forget.

# Remains of a Story

A cloud-touched tower;
a shining rope of hair.

\* \* \* \*

Armies marching
across continents.

\* \* \* \*

A whispering: "history is grief"

\* \* \* \*

The ravishment
of my soul in the dark wood,
the searing torrent

of divine light
sudden and saving
on the negative road.

\* \* \* \*

A guitar singing of
the distance of stars.

\* \* \* \*

Where to begin
with all that we wanted?

# ANOTHER BEGINNING

To the coppery provinces
of sigh and sneer
the last raucous ghosts
have shambled back,
leaving me to my own
ceremony of departure.
The unaccustomed quiet
startles my heart up from
its bloodshot crouch
over the bog-hole
of resentments to catch
the wind's new tang. And
my song flexes
its lemon fingers, takes up
the lovely fiddle it had
unstrung, and strikes
the crazy phrasings of assent,
as if I had never stopped
believing this good boat
would be waiting
and the passage paid in full.

# THE HUNT

"*From how many clearings,
into how many nights*

*have I looked and smelled
Orion and his dogs*

*slow foot after slow foot
cross the terrible sky.*

*How often has my heart worn
his dagger of stars*

*as someone dark as earth
parted the branches*

*and looked into me
the girl to whom he told his love,*

*and I looked back for an instant
with her wild, pained eyes
and fled, grazed by the mystery.*"

# Aubade

All I have to say
is this, she says, or she says
nothing, or a few words
about nothing.

What she needs, she says,
is this, and not much
of that at that; enough
she says is enough.

Since this is what she says
I say (I have to say)
what she needs to have
said-- nothing or almost or

this this this,
as this: this green spike of light
this morning entering between
the bedroom curtains turned

your skin to oceans
of green anemones,
now blowing this way,
now this, then this,

and this, and this, and this.

# A Dream Is Its Own Significance

Out of the ground
a tilling sound--
dull suck of struck clay,

and all of me came
from years around
to pass the rhythm's day.

I was a field
of dancing clowns
ringing a field of pain,

and punch-drunk sower,
and overseer
flashing his club in the rain.

Not Joseph himself
could be happier
hearing the split of the husk,

the glug of the flask,
the mesh of the flesh,
the fiddles flown out of the dusk:

Oh, a dream is its own
significance,
as full and as null as a stone,

and the drums in the sleep
all beat the same beat
as the sea rolling over a bone.

# EATING SILVER

(for Saba Hussain Qizilbash)
In the aroma of things that keep body and soul
together-- potatoes, green
chilis, garlic, carrots,
and fifty everyday spices--
a story about foods
from your homeland
dipped in pure silver.

Would eating
silver be like swallowing
your bracelet of little hearts,
I unable to imagine
a less substantial form?
And would day
after day, eating silver, our
faces grow into mirrors,
or even our hearts?

But later you give me to eat
a cardamom seed coated
with the thinnest silver foil
I roll on my tongue
and bite. And in my voice begin
the first tremblings
of a tiny bell cast
in the kingdom of miracles.

# II

# CHEMICAL WEDDING

Everything is a metaphor. I myself am a myth about myself; for is it not as a myth that I hasten to this tryst?

*—Kierkegaard*

# The Purpose of a Sonnet
# in a Time of Chaos

For weeks he had been thinking about forms,
gaunt trees in the garden, a winterkilled fawn
his dog clawed from the snow, and, obsessively,
in his wife's absence, the form of his own desire--
He drank much of the night and suspected
therefore that what he gained in her body
was some temporary oblivion.
This was not a form of love and he was terrified.

He spent the mornings cataloging
his grandfather's papers on mathematics,
and it was in a draft of the famous essay
"Reality and the Approximate
Solutions to Differential Equations"
he found an unsent letter to a woman
in France which, among the many "O"s and "amour"s
and "ange"s, contained a sonnet in English.

He read:
   *I might have passed my life with hardened heart*
   *Toying with beauteous forms inside my head*
   *If they sweet form fresh sprung from Nature's art*
   *Had not my blind eyes seized and openéd.*
   *In thee my manly powers regain their source*
   *As flesh the chill of winter casts away*
   *And in full sun forgets about remorse*
   *And sings out gaily "Let us seize the day".*
   *Oh that our lives forever might be one*
   *Is my one wish and chief of my desires,*

*For in the nights when I must lie alone*
*Not death itself could pain as do those fires*
*Burning inside my body and my dreams--*
*Thou the quenching spark, the blazing stream!*

Dec. 1940

At first he smiled at the amateurish poem, but
reading it again and remembering
the aloof, proper man his grandfather seemed,
and recalling the long after-dinner discussions
about he limits of reason, and the functions
of art in the Age of Science, he was
aware suddenly of the mind as some small
cowering thing hiding itself inside
geometry and machines and philosophy
while the world lurched and crumbled.

Could a man, he wondered, be
summarized in a poem, his whole soul
spill out its nature in a meager moment
of structured time?

                    He stood by the picture-window
in the warm study.  Snow was falling
through his reflection.  He saw how thin he was
with longing for his wife and wondered
if inside the forms of love a thin man
frightened by himself and by a time
of chaos could save his soul from oblivion.

# I.

We live in the anonymous exactions
of our energies; or perhaps more,
in the slow, considered diffusions
of...call it virtù.  Let us be frank, I tell her,
the way you read me, I too read you:
And so, *semblablée*, *soeur*, sincere one,
consider how today the lithe new
campaniles of the foxgloves have flung
their extravagant music to the breeze,
and red-winged blackbirds, like rows of acolytes,
rained their feverish hosannahs through the leaves.
It was, it was-- spring's surfeit cast across limits,
there, gratuitous, only to accept;
not symbol, not metaphor, not text.

## II.

Shells, emptied, given up in the scouring
drag of sand, studded the beach like bone
fragments from a thousand wars.  And then
seeing the dunes dense with salal unraveling
to luminous boas of ocean mist
bereavement heaved within me and I was conscious
of an endless interchange with otherness
defining me through everything I've lost.

Don't you know, I tell her, I crave identity
beyond the grind of time, something to comprehend
our brief replenishing of each other?
Won't you cleave to me that flesh of your body
with mine might be one and tensile, withstand
with me the intrinsic absences I fear we are?

# III.

"I lay face down in the wet, carnal loam;
the dusky furrows opened under me
as though my presence animated some
stony presence that grasped me hungrily.

"Cries from an anonymous core as I came
up from my own darkness; I smelt the sea
washing along my flesh, an acrid, warm
spill I couldn't tell if into or out of me:

"That was it! A raging thirst for validation
by something breathing and elemental,
the fantasies of a starving will
desiring only its own creations;

"As, every time I dreamt of you, the shades
of every other woman stalked and would not fade."

# IV.

Curlews keep opening a rift in my sleep,
tremulous nocturnes of distance.  Is it
exile to be anywhere dreaming of what's
beyond, beyond, as once I hoped against hope
for revolution, for universal spleen?
One night when the cries came over the fields
I was suddenly heart deep in the old
country of desperate remedies, grown
sly with subversion, trying such words
as "I have plummeted the dark tunnel
of a bird's call and met my fundamental
self at the end.  Though the passage is hard,
we can be everywhere at home in everything".
She said I woke her up with my screaming.

# V.

Morning.  A wailing zoom between sleeping
and waking, and a panic back along
the long road of a dream.  The hills are bristling
with chainsaws gouging their pained jags of song
from a green silence. Why does it resonate
in the hollow of my will with pure
hardness, a granite vein concealed beneath
the plausive susurrus of leaves?  I hear
someone unleash a bitter laughter
and say "Would you have me call you Light-foot,
praise your gentle ways with goddamn dryads,
your delicate siftings?  I know you better,
I saw your lust for plunder in my own head,
the things you said you'd die for, kill for . . ."

# VI.

Circle, clearing, places where I'm not
the forgetter of details, sentimental
drunk, or the quick, unreliable
promiser of worlds, is where we meet,
the light lunar, alkali, reeling
with shadows, and I the hesitant, wooed one
stepping from my body and unbinding
words like tresses, saying "Here I am".
And it must be that after our wild
trysts, our tangling swirling emptinesses
I carry away from you a seed, cold
but on fire, of an order that is
of the blood and stars together, the complete
union hungering to sunder, then repeat . . .

III

# No Second Heaven

Die Welt is fort, ich muß dich tragen
—*Paul Celan*

# EITHER / OR

### 1. *The Sowing Fiddle*

Beyond the invisible hills,
in the great towns' market squares
in red skirts and frills
bears are turning slow reels

to the songs ground
out of barrel-organs
by the morose, bony hands
of bewildered apes.  The sounds

carry on the bituminous air,
the catches and wheezes,
all the way here, here
to my acres' soft floor

where I execute gavottes
in the heady musks
of Jack-In-The-Pulpit
and Rich Man's Margaret.

So, I'll hum you these tunes--
"Ruth In The Cornfield",
"The Lovers And The Loons"--
across my knees I'll play spoons

of stolen gold, and from the hump

of my shoulders I'll fling wheat-seeds
and weed-seeds and jump
through haysheds with my flaming lamp.

And over the black hills, in fours
and threes, the hulking bears
will stumble and the sad apes bray
such music as would wring tears

from a rainbow.  And all their crippled works
I'll gather to the keeping of my wild park
and saw my sowing fiddle
dawn to dark.


2. *The Singing Sword*

in every broken place   monuments are raised
beginning with he places   you should   be able
to know   as your own   as when a tunnel
caved open   in my   mother's heart
she placed a statue   of Saint Jude
right in the rift   a cheap plastic figure
with a night   light   flickering before him
I've   done   something similar   many
times   as when in the brooding   absence   that was my
father   I   put   an ice-sculpture
to the god of silence   that still   hangs
on there   and later   as I   learned to love
sincerely   with my body   and it was not
enough   I poured   libations of wine   into
the raw tear   between   the girl   and me

we   hide   our violence
our diversions   under simulacra and effigies
many millions of them   death-squads
plant little torches   for democracy
in the bullet   holes   in the skulls
of men   of women   who are   like them

young men   from Mississippi   from Iowa
sing war   songs   at the edge   of a jungle
or a desert       they lust   for dying and death
they have     learned   to put   gods and monuments   wherever
fractures   open   things that conceal
even as they   bless   the gap   of the wound

it is because of this   you hear
sometimes   a man sits down   outside
a mansion   don't kill for me   police   appear
beat   him up   take   him   away
a woman chains   her self   to the revolving door
of   her children   black   with cancer   a doctor   comes
every time it happens
you can hear   the scranneling
monuments   effigies   statues
chipped at   hacked at   hammered at
the notes   of steel on stone   steel in air
holding persisting joining
it is neither a joyous   nor beautiful song
this song of strength   of frailty   of swords
unsheathed   from our own   steady humanness
to flash   in our own   steady dark
but all we have to quicken   the dead air
all we have to quicken   keep it

# COLUMBUS

The simple trees
open an aisle

down which the pylons arrive, a shimmering
ambassadorial procession

taking the hills in its stride
and claiming the valley for a higher power.

The power-lines reach all the way
back to Christopher Columbus,

a dank oubliette in the heart
of old Europe where he spits his prayers:

Blazing caravels lift towards the stars
with the zeal of angels.

"We have cross", they report, "the edge of the world,
and from this distance, this thrumming space,

the earth behind us is completely dark".

# MACHINE

After the rain,
                in twos
and threes, down
                by the dark
stagnant
        pond, the frogs
unroll
through the water-
weeds long
            quivering ribbons
of extruded
                Air, until
with the sky's vault
already (Such sound!
                    Such sound!)
creaking and cracking they
all
   together
            stop

# Voyage of the Beagle

Clock-towers no longer chime
with celestial self-importance,
but sputter a panicked ringing over
London roofs.  Queen Victoria's
annual procession betrays
its lack of confidence
by a smoother rigidity and timing
more exact than usual.
                        The carriage-horses
strain in their tinkling harnesses,
the grimed, flinty children wave their flags
and cheer, and above, on the balconied crescents
of white town-houses, men in morning suits
pull on fresh cigars.
                        Chambermaids pass on
the cross-shaped birthmarks of their owners'
belt-buckles on their lean thighs.
The wilder ark  pitches through
oceans under the broken music of dancing stars.

# In Snow Country

Snow is ghosting
out of a sky
the color of snow
and the cursive script
of pine and fir is blanked and tattered
by an overlay of white.

It is Christmas
and I have walked
away from the house, from
the radio cackling its jingles
and acronyms through
a hush of static.

I brush snow from a tree stump,
sit, and try to think
what it could mean for words
to be nerved to the body
like the whole sense of touch,
to stretch the voice
out like a hand and fingers
and grasp "war" and "love" and "fear".

Everything is silent--
the snow makes no sound
piling on the earth.
And as the air grows colder
I jump up and down
beating my hands together
to set the blood moving
into my growing numbness.

# Lorca Leaving

Reapers are strumming the burnt fields
without a sound and the stunned fennel
on the hillside is misting into
the bronze air.  There is a snowy peacock
singing in the ruined orange tree
by my window, a journeying song,
a journeying song.  And I have risen
from a shadow's green hands and green kisses
to walk away from this shimmering house.

O heaving country where my grief expends
itself in the harness bells of blue-black
horses and moonslicked women in their wedding
skirts of river foam, we are of one flesh
and I forget nothing.  In the angled arms
of The City Without A Name someone
waits to teach me in the tongue of white
and the tongue of ash the wild plums,
the coalstone proverbs, arias of the salmon,
the one-eyed street girl with her rose.

Now while the horns of solitary bonfires
pour their mourning in the turquoise font
of that other sky, tell me we lose nothing
in the crossing over but the habit
of a voice's cracked pitch, tell me
how once the fishermen of Cadiz heard
their fathers sing inside the yellow star
Arcturus, a severe, searing, beautiful song
of nets and canvas, tell me before
this ashen snow breaking from my own eyes
hardens over the ground of memory
like a carapace, a mirror, nothing I know.

# About Time

Decantations of golden boy
in a chalice of bone, nightcaps
fit for divinity; pigeon-coos
on the breeze, and the moon, and the moss;
prince of a vertical Jerusalem
in your eye.

You must have left the lamp on
for the family ghosts, afraid of your life
of the dark.  Look at me, will you,
all aglow, mining for light
in the depths of the snow
and nobody home.

How much further when you're this far gone?
Can you gather enough wind
for the walk on, for, say it now,
some desperate beauty
supine on the white plane
of its own passing;

and the dead up to their eyes
in the dead?

# PROPHECY

The days, as they get away, seem to spiral
down to a place of unmitigated white
located precisely between systole
and diastole in the heat's unrelenting song
of soon, soon.
     It's not that I lose
memories or consequences, but the fine
details, the smell of a pear halved and left
out overnight on a blue plate, the thread
starting to unravel on the topmost button
of that blouse she bought in Italy; you know
what I mean.
     All morning at the field's edge
I've been piling old stumps and brushwood
on a roaring fire, my mind wandering
in the tortuous Greek of *Revelations*,
my hands working and praying without me:

Και  ειδον θρόνον μέγαν λευκον

*"And I saw a great white throne and the one
who sat on it; the earth and the heaven
fled from his presence and no place was found for them"*
  Moment by moment this is how it happens,
and will happen.

# THE SWAN

The moment
you fold around yourself
that bellowing body of air
and drop,
you hear her opening her own name
to find a shaft there
deeper than herself,
dark, echoing,
full of the sacrifices,
the languages, the bees,
and at the end
the pool where nothing is
clear, where rumors of you
rise into her shriek; you
never intended
anything, not
even this, this arc
of departure
that takes you over
a village of eyes,
not even your reflection
that lights on and consoles
the chaos waking beneath you.

# A Hearty Welcome to
# the Antichrist

Walking through the woods behind my house I came upon a
flock of passenger pigeons settled in the bare trees like
pink flowers. When I asked what they were doing in such an
unlikely roost they replied in one voice "Nous sommes les
anges de les anges à venir; priez pour nous, pour nous, pour
nous".

My friend Aurora interprets dreams for a living. Because
everything is something else and not itself she studiously
draws connections between words and their shadows. "French",
she muses; "la langue Francaise, la longue francaise; ange,
angine; that repeated 'nous'; pigeon, pige...Are things
becoming clear?" It wasn't a dream, I tell her.

At night the trees rattle inside the darkness. In Summer
they hiss, or rather, shiss, like waves retreating to the
ocean. Unleaved, leaved; absent, present; and in between?
Prepositions, floating adverbs, trial pronouns.

(Examples:)

After death the self metastasizes into its constituent
illusions which appear to the soul as monstrous images.

I am the fingers of a black bamboo snatching at the wind.

The Government has banned your last book because of the
essay entitled 'The Cunt of Jesus Is A Fishy Concept'. How
do you feel about it?

(End of examples)

Aurora tells me this story: When you lived in Paris you were
unbearably lonely (cf.nous), so, one night, desperate
for human contact, you made your way to a bordello and
paid for a girl (cf. pigeon, pige). Improbably, she was
angelic looking, a tall, gentle girl you felt you could fall
in love with in other circumstances; but there, in
that place, at that time, you started to treat the
situation as, so to speak, experiential capital,
something you could store up and write about later (cf.
pige). Now, years later, the fact that the possibility
of her love is forever lost to you makes you sick at heart
(cf. ange, angine), and your memory of how in your past
behaviour, both in sexual and moral terms, you were untrue
to yourself, reveals both an unresolved relationship to the
religious sources of your morality (cf. priez) and a
suspicion that you might not have developed sufficient inner
strength to act any better in the future (cf. à venir).

I insist it is not a dream.

Think. Jesus said that in the End Times there would be many
signs, and have there ever been so many signs? But even
still, O ye of little faith, you demand interpretations, as
though consistency were a guarantee of truth. Do you not
remember that morning on the mountainside when He said that
plausibility is the enemy of prophecy, and He cursed the
name of Jester Joseph, and held up in His hand a stone of
the ground which instantly shrieked? It didn't mean
anything, He said, it simply was.

What, for example, could this mean?

When the Pope came to Dublin he threw a stone in the Liffey,
saying that if it floated he'd go back home. The assembled
multitude prayed for a miracle not to happen and it didn't,

so he stayed. The throng surged behind the Pope's glass
coach singing their 'Te Deums', and as the crowd flowed down
O'Connell Street a hunched old man suddenly jumped out in
front of the procession holding a placard with the words "A
Hearty Welcome To The Antichrist". Before he was trampled to
death, he and the Pope exchanged knowing winks. End of
example.

Now the strange thing is I live in the heart of a city (pick
a city, any city), so there are no woods within fifteen
miles. There are, however, "whole forests of" (metaphor)
traffic lights, stop signs, pedestrian lights, street signs,
shop signs, billboards, sandwichboards, advertising blimps,
loudspeakers and video screens. And it is there, Yea, even
among such as these, that I have spoken with the angels of
the coming angels.

(Is this true?) (  □ Yes     □ No     Choose One)

At night the trees rattle inside the darkness. (You may now
revise your choice). At dawn we gather together, my wife, my
children, my dogs, my cattle, and I, and partake of the
feast.

Here is the recipe: Take as many pigeons as there are
persons in the catacomb and dredge them in spiced flour.
Sauté the birds in butter until they are seared and place
them in a pot. Keep the grease in the frying pan and cook
chopped onions and carrots in it; add half a cup of water
per person. Pour all of this over the birds in the pot and
cover. Roast in an oven at 350 degrees for an hour, then serve on
a dish of boiled mushrooms and potatoes. Eat and wait.

So what are you/we waiting for?

The bright phosphorescent mills are dancing in the air
of the planet America (as was foretold).

We begin to begin again, again (as was foretold).
There is only one story (as was foretold).
There is only one dream (as was foretold).
You are in complete control (as was foretold).

Yesterday, inevitably, I took Aurora to bed as the final
stage of my talking cure, and today she handed me a love
poem (love!) called "Last Words":

> *Feet mangled by frost, starting to rot,*
> *Holding up the progress*
> *Of Captain Scott,*
>
> *He made his decision, raised the flap—*
> *"I'm going outside and may be some time"—*
> *He almost strode from the bivouac.*
>
> *But in these last words of Captain Oates*
> *There are dangerous questions*
> *For prophets and poets—*
>
> *Who was it left? Who was it stayed?*
> *Did all of them die*
> *Or was somebody saved?*

Behind my eyes the bones of passenger pigeons strike like
trees into the open sky.
What is the word for this?

Cloudbursts of digital rain fall on the villages of the
damned.
What is the word for this?

You are in control; go on,
What is the word?

# Accusation

Behind you spreads
the shimmer of human-
shaped air, and you would not
look back though your life
depends on all
the columns of cries rising
in smoke, though you must know
these rags of beseeching
taken up and scattered
in your wake are all
that makes it through
from the place where
you knelt kissing the lilies.

# LETTER FROM IRELAND

You ask again about my life: I have been walking
for weeks out of its botched shape, wading across
fields, looking for signs unfettered from proverb,
omen, superstition. I'd love to send you
news that would keep on going clear as a bell
between one day and the next, but I have none
that hasn't swelled grievously into the wreckage
of understanding before I knew it.
Around here the fishermen turn on their heels
if they see a fox before reaching the boat-slip--
I buy them pints so they'll tell me things like this
as though they believed them. They're lost
as I am.
       And the other morning I saw
in the gap where an old field wall has fallen
nettles spill through to the road's scutched margin.
I took notice of them for the first time
because they had come into delicate flower,
raised white throats to the air out of the wet green
overnight. Later, a neighbour who still plucks them
for soup told me the nettle used to be
the most beautiful plant in Paradise
until the serpent hid beneath it
after tempting Eve; and she also said
some people call them *archangels*; in any case
they taste good, boiled with carrots and onions.
Do you hear my sadness in this?
                 It all
falls through me like sand draining through some

ignorant hand, the sweep of a maybe-maybe-
not smile rainbowing all over this place.
                                        Is
this what you wanted to know, then, about
how I'm keeping these days, at home
and not at home, worrying myself
well by walking, walking on, poking
and prodding at the seams of the meaning
with whatever turns up? It's the same old
obsession with me, wanting my life to be pure
abandonment of all that's thrown together
for consolation, wanting instead
the good silence on the other side
of truths.
                    And you, in your life, how are you?

# Manuscript Illumination

Desperation's snowblinding weather,
cleared only by the meadowlark's supple persistence
igniting in a fine-boned alder:

this is a life's stubborn margin
to the times' indefatigable mumble,
everything not given up or given up on.

To see myself, then, as one of the worriers
cobbled out of the best that's been repressed,
poised aslant to whatever neat *historia*:

hawk-headed, a briary, prehensile tongue,
body of a lion, mountain-goat's hooves,
and the sturdy, seraphic wings:

more rampant now ignorance blunts the uncials
and prophecies are fulfilled in dreams
unplummetted by any event's warning-bell.

As for that meadowlark, she might spiral
another string of praise from what's left
of the day and watch it weave and curl

effortlessly into the truth:
*In principio erat verbum.*
What is it you haven't been told?

# Signs Following

Of the closed fist that yet
can snare a hawk what is
there to understand
of a luck like the river of air
shriven to the river of water
or the night always
unspooling horses and wings?
This is where we are given
to start from, all
the rest being the sad
paws of gravity striking
or not: Don't you hear
it drawing up out
of each other's lonely wells
some answering cry, howl,
moan, sigh, laugh or even word, river
to our rivers, blessing
on our stony names? We might
dream all the centuries
of books will run out
of the hunter's moon's eyes like salt
but what I am telling you
will put a cut branch of wild
olives in our fear's thatch,
start in us the chance that is
the impossible fruiting again
and again.
           I do not know
how I know this, this

truest of absurdities
in the world, but,
here, close your hand
and I will find you all
you never needed
from me-- a jewel
of hope in your palm.

# TARA

Let yourself down by the string
that keeps your tongue tied
to your mouth's civil floor,
down where the dark is green
as the river you have always half-
remembered. Meath, Bhutan,
somewhere someone is opening
herself up to you like a flower,
or a leaf, or a flower, for there
is nowhere she cannot hear
the passion drumming
on the ribs of your poem:

*Om* meaning a hill in Ireland,
*Om* meaning an ibex horn,
*Om* meaning yes, meaning now, meaning home.
Yes, *Om* meaning yes, meaning home.

The prayer of home.

# FEVER

At  4a.m. the fabulous village roosters
hang their hearts on the last stars;

the bat-eared dogs call over the roofs
and in my dream someone sharpens a bird-blue knife.

I have pushed across the lake on a boat
all planks and angles like a cobbled gate

to fling back my necklace of rusty verbs.
My throat unravels into shiny barbs.

I slash the sky until it rains—
forty days and forty nights my bones

vibrate and turn. And Santa Catarina,
San Antonio beat a slow, slow marimba

for the *curandera* dancing on my pillow,
humming *maybe tomorrow, maybe tomorrow.*

Santa Catarina Palopó, Guatemala.

# WHITE MOUNTAINS, NEW HAMPSHIRE

Everything I say
falls back on me
like rain's
slow erosion. The mountain
thrush opens
her aria of tender
admonishing
as though I am
her child: empty,
empty your hands; what is there
to carry
into the winter?
not a name,
not a blessing,
not even the emptiest
words on the earth
*moose . . . Indian*

# About the Author

Ger Killeen's previous books include *A Wren*, which won the 1989 Bluestem Award for Poetry, and *A Stone That Will Leap Over The Waves* (Trask House Books, 1999).

His work has been anthologized in *From Here We Speak* (OSU Press), *On the Counterscarp* (Salmon Publishing), and *American Poetry: The Next Generation* (Carnegie-Mellon University Press).

Killeen lives on the Oregon coast and is a professor in the Dept. of English Literature & Writing at Marylhurst University.

www.ingramcontent.com/pod-product-compliance
Lightning Source LLC
Chambersburg PA
CBHW032028090426
42741CB00006B/778